Deadly History

THE VIKINGS

RAIDS OF TERROR AND BLOODY BATTLES

CHERITON
CHILDREN'S BOOKS

Published in 2023 by **Cheriton Children's Books**
1 Bank Drive West, Shrewsbury, Shropshire, SY3 9DJ, UK

© 2023 Cheriton Children's Books

First Edition

Authors: Sarah Eason and Louise Spilsbury
Designer: Paul Myerscough
Editor: Deborah Jones
Proofreader: Suzanne Gifford

Printed in China

Please visit our website,
www.cheritonchildrensbooks.com
to see more of our high-quality books.

CONTENTS

CHAPTER 1

VIKING TERROR

The Vikings were scary warriors who set sail from **Scandinavia**, an area in Northern Europe. They were focused on winning fame and fortune. From 700 CE to 1100 CE, the Vikings struck fear into the hearts of many people around the coasts of Europe and beyond.

Simple to Spine-Chilling

The early Vikings were quiet, peaceful people who lived a simple life. They spent their days farming and fishing. They made a living from the land and the cold seas that they lived near.

The word "Viking" comes from the **Norse** word for a pirate raid.

Ships and Stealing

The tales of terror about the Vikings began when they built ships that could carry them far from their coastal homes. They developed a taste for stealing treasure in spine-chilling raids, and had no problems fighting and killing anyone who stood in their way.

Viking helmets were often made from pieces of iron that were fixed together. A helmet was the most important thing that a Viking owned. Wearing one in battle could mean the difference between living and dying.

Viking helmets were made of strong, thick iron and were very heavy. They weighed up to 9 pounds (4 kg).

Easier Elsewhere

Being a Viking farmer in Scandinavia was very challenging, so it is not surprising that the Vikings decided to look for an easier way to survive, and started raiding foreign lands for treasure.

Indoor Living

The long, dark winters in Scandinavia were cold and harsh, so farm animals such as cows had to be kept indoors. A Viking home was called a longhouse and it had just one room for all the family to share with its animals.

Farming in Viking times was hard work in an often-bleak landscape, and only the eldest son could **inherit** the farm when a father died. This, along with the general hardships of life in Viking lands, tempted younger brothers to go elsewhere to get farmland of their own.

Leaving for a New Life

Farming on icy lands near the Arctic was difficult. Everything had to be done by hand, so life was tough and required a lot of hard, constant work. Many Vikings left their homeland in search of better land to farm. Others left to fight and find treasure.

Dark and Deadly!

Viking boys were not only expected to work on the farm—they had to train as warriors, too. Viking boys were taught to fight using spears, swords, and axes.

This is a reconstruction of a Viking longhouse. Everyone slept, ate, and did indoor work inside the longhouse.

Raids That Paid

The Vikings first raided England in 793 CE. With little opposition from the poor people they attacked, the Vikings found the raid easy. After it proved successful, the Vikings developed a taste for blood! They began to send out vicious gangs of raiders to places far and wide.

Killing and Stealing

Viking raids were violent and deadly. A gang of Vikings would arrive at a place by boat and attack the towns and villages along the coast or next to rivers. They stole treasures such as gold, jewels, and coins. They killed anyone who tried to stop them.

Iona Abbey off the coast of Scotland was first attacked by Viking raiders in 795 CE, and then again in 802, 806, and 825 CE. At the raid in 806 CE, the Vikings killed 68 **monks** from the abbey. Seeing a Viking raider for the first time must have been terrifying for the monks.

A Life of Slavery

Vikings also kidnapped people on their raids and made them into **slaves**. They forced slaves to do the hardest, dirtiest jobs on their farms and in their villages. If a slave misbehaved, they were badly beaten. If a slave tried to run away, he or she could be brutally killed.

Dark and Deadly!

Most Vikings were very mean to their slaves. Not only did they make them work hard, they also gave them rude and horrible names such as Sluggard, Stumpy, and Lout!

WHY DO YOU THINK THE VIKINGS KILLED SLAVES WHO TRIED TO RUN AWAY? WHAT EFFECT DO YOU THINK THAT MAY HAVE HAD ON OTHER SLAVES?

Vikings kept their slaves in chains and heavy iron collars to keep them from escaping.

CHAPTER 2

SLIT-THROAT SAILORS

The Vikings ruled the sea because they had the sleekest ships of the age. The Vikings sailed in **lethal** longships. These strong ships carried them quickly and safely across stormy North Atlantic waves, to attack unsuspecting people in faraway lands.

Longships were not only wide and stable, but also light and fast. These qualities made them formidable.

Longship Labor

Making longships was a tough, unpleasant job. Large wooden planks had to be cut, held in place, and nailed by hand. Then, to make the ships watertight, workers had to fill in the spaces between the planks with animal hair mixed with tar and grease.

Rowing to Raid

Longships had one large woolen sail, but if the wind dropped, the Vikings had around 50 oars to keep up their speed. The rowers' hands became so blistered that the Vikings rubbed smelly fish oil on them to reduce **friction** and prevent painful chafing.

Dark and Deadly!

At the front of most Viking longships was the shape of a creature, such as a scary-looking dragon, carved in wood. When people saw the monster on the front of an approaching ship, they must have been terrified.

Viking longships were often known as dragon ships because of their **menacing** dragon **figureheads**.

Tough for Vikings

There is no doubt that the Vikings were terrifying. They brought fear and horror to the lands they raided. However, life on board the longships was not easy for the Vikings—in fact, it was full of hardships.

Miserable Meals

At sea, the Vikings could not risk setting fire to their precious wooden boats by cooking their meals, so their food was mainly cold and made up of chewy dried fish or meat. For drink, the Vikings had water, beer, or sour milk.

Not a Good Night's Sleep

Longships had no covered areas, so Viking warriors mostly slept in the open on the hard, wooden deck. They had only blankets or furs for shelter and warmth. Sometimes, they went ashore, where they slept under woolen tents and lit fires to cook food and keep warm.

Viking sailors had to be tough. They faced huge waves and icy cold water in longships like this one.

Dark and Deadly!

One especially horrible Viking meal was **fermented** shark meat. This was made by urinating on dead fish, then burying it underground. **Bacteria** then got to work on the fish and made it rot.

Fermented shark meat is made from Greenland sharks, which are common in Scandinavian waters.

LIFE AT SEA WAS FULL OF HARDSHIPS. SO WHY DO YOU THINK THE VIKINGS WERE PREPARED TO ENDURE IT?

Sneaky Surprises

Viking longships were made to travel quickly. They were also made to stay intact on dangerous seas. But they were also designed for another reason—to creep up rivers so the Vikings could spring sudden violent raids on unsuspecting villagers.

Not so Safe

Longships were very shallow so that they could travel in water only 3 feet (1 m) deep. This meant they could be used to travel up rivers to **settlements** where people thought they were safe from attack by ship. They could also run straight onto a beach or up a shallow river bank.

Big but Light

Longships were very light for their size. They had parts that could be quickly removed so the Vikings could drag the ships overland to get to a nearby river. That meant they did not have to sail out to sea again.

Raiding by river gave the Vikings a huge advantage. Their ships could be quickly hauled out of the water and onto land during a raid.

Dark and Deadly!

Easy-to-maneuver boats allowed the bloodthirsty Vikings to take a village by surprise. When they arrived at their destination, they quickly jumped out and attacked before their victims had time to defend themselves.

The Vikings moved from river to river, carrying and dragging their boats overland.

CHAPTER 3

WIELDING WEAPONS

The Vikings loved a good fight! These fierce people were so deadly, and their raids so hard to resist, because they wielded murderous weapons. And the vicious Vikings used them with a terrifying savagery.

Scary Spear-Throwers

The Viking spear was an iron blade on a wooden pole and was up to 9 feet (3 m) long. The Vikings could throw two spears at a time using both hands, or even catch an enemy spear as it flew toward them, and then throw it back with deadly accuracy.

It must have been terrifying to witness a Viking warrior charging forward while wielding a weapon.

Armed with Axes

Viking axes were lethal. They had wide, curved blades or blades shaped like sharp spikes, and long handles. They were used to cut enemies with heavy blows and were also thrown. A warrior with a large ax would often take cover behind the front line of a gang of Vikings and then rush out to attack **opponents** when he was close enough.

Dark and Deadly!

Viking shields were hooked onto the sides of a longship. When the ship pulled up onto land, the warriors could grab them quickly and jump out to begin their deadly attack.

Strong, circular shields were made of wood and iron and were up to 3 feet (1 m) wide.

Super Swords

To a Viking, his greatest weapon was his sword. Swords were usually the most expensive object that a Viking owned. They were also the deadliest and most efficient of all the Viking weapons.

Light and Flexible

Swords were strong, but also light and able to bend. This meant that the Vikings could hold them in one hand while in the other hand they held a shield. Sword handles were often made of bone, **antler**, or precious metals such as gold and silver.

Viking swords were expensive to make, so owning one was a sign of wealth and status. The swords were often passed down generations, from father to son, as prized possessions.

Dark and Deadly!

Viking swords were so deadly that the Vikings often gave them bloodcurdling names, such as Viper, Gnawer, Flame of Battle, Hole-Maker, and Leg-Biter.

Fighting a Viking was dangerous simply because their swords were superior to their victims'. Viking steel swords were less likely to break and lose their sharpness in battle than their victims' iron ones.

WHAT DO YOU THINK WE CAN LEARN FROM THE NAMES THAT VIKINGS GAVE THEIR SWORDS?

Sharp and Deadly

Swords could be 3 feet (1 m) long and were usually double-edged. Both edges of the blade were very sharp and equally dangerous. A warrior carried his sword in a leather holder that hung from his waist, so that he could pull it out quickly in a fight.

Crazily Scary

Warriors called berserkers were the most terrifying of all. These Vikings wore bearskins, believing that they would give them the strength and terror of a bear. Berserkers believed they did not need to wear battle armor because Odin, the Viking god of war, gave them superpowers.

No-Pain Zone

The berserkers sometimes fought in gangs that all went into battle in the same terrifying way. They were bloodthirsty, had no fear for their own life, and ignored the pain of wounds. They worked themselves into a frenzy so intense it is said they howled like wild animals and bit on the edges of their shields out of pure rage!

Padded Out

Viking leaders wore long tunics of iron **chain mail** to protect themselves from enemy weapons. Most Vikings wore padded leather shirts to absorb the impact of arrow or sword strikes.

Beserkers often fought bare-chested, having no fear of any pain from the battle to come. The berserkers were among the most feared of all Vikings.

Dark and Deadly!

The word "berserk" means out of control. It comes from the Viking word for the fierce warriors named berserkers, who fought with an uncontrollable fury.

This Viking chess piece shows a wild-eyed berserker biting the top of his shield.

CHAPTER 4

HIT AND RUN

The Vikings made hit-and-run raids on cities and towns along any coasts they could reach by ship. Their deadly attacks spread fear like wildfire across Europe. No word inspired more terror than Viking.

Monastery Mayhem

The Vikings first raided England in 793 CE. During this raid they attacked a **monastery** in northern England called Lindisfarne. The monks living there had no weapons and they did not even try to fight back. The Vikings burned down their buildings, chased the monks into the sea to drown, and stole their treasure.

Vikings often sailed through the night to be able to land their ships at dawn and launch a surprise attack.

THE MONKS PUT UP NO FIGHT AGAINST THE VIKINGS. WHAT EFFECT DO YOU THINK THAT MAY HAVE HAD ON THE VIKINGS AND THEIR FUTURE RAIDS?

Treasure Stash

Vikings destroyed the monastery at Lindisfarne. Monasteries were perfect targets for the Vikings because they had no defenses and the monks did not fight back. The Vikings could easily take the valuable treasure inside the buildings. Having their ships nearby also meant that they could quickly stash everything they stole, then make a speedy getaway.

Dark and Deadly!

During raids, the Vikings would leap from boats, scream battle cries, and storm through buildings. They even murdered villagers while they were still asleep in their beds.

Valuable **manuscripts** were stolen from the monasteries.

Gang Warfare

A gang of vicious Vikings must have been terrifying for anyone who saw them. They would have struck fear into the hearts of any victim. The Vikings traveled far and wide to **plunder** and kill with ever-bigger forces.

Paris Prisoners

In 845 CE, 120 boats carrying up to 4,000 Viking warriors sailed up the Seine River to attack Paris, France. They were met by two French forces. The Vikings finished off one quickly, then they took more than 200 prisoners, and hanged them on the riverbank to frighten off any remaining French opponents.

Paid to Leave

After the Vikings had defeated the French, they demanded treasure. The French king was so terrified of the Viking warriors that he handed over a fortune in gold and silver to make the fearsome fighters go away.

Viking warriors may have marked their faces with frightening makeup to terrify their victims even further.

This illustration shows Viking ships sailing toward the walls of Paris.

Dark and Deadly!

To make themselves look even scarier, Viking raiders filed their teeth into sharp points or cut grooves into them. They also rubbed red berry juice onto teeth so that they looked more bloodthirsty.

Scary Settlers

After years of spreading terror, stealing treasures, and kidnapping slaves, the Vikings decided not only to raid places, but also to **conquer** them. They wanted to put down roots in the places they attacked.

All-Out War

In 865 CE, the Vikings went from raiders to **invaders** when they tried to conquer England. The Vikings gathered a great army and set out on ships to wage total war on **Anglo-Saxon** kingdoms. They fought fierce battles at sea and destroyed lands. They murdered many people and soon, the Vikings had conquered most of England.

Bloody Fights

Vicious battles were fought between Viking armies who roamed the countryside and the English defenders. Hundreds of people were brutally killed and fields were stained with blood. Eventually, most areas were brought back under English control, but not before the Vikings had established several of their own cities and settlements.

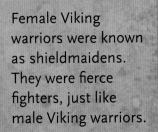

Female Viking warriors were known as shieldmaidens. They were fierce fighters, just like male Viking warriors.

Dark and Deadly!

There is evidence that fierce female Vikings fought alongside men. Bodies of badly injured female fighters have been found beside male Vikings in warrior graves.

These remains were discovered in a **mass grave** of dead Vikings from the great army found in England.

CHAPTER 5

GRUESOME GODS

The Vikings believed in a number of terrifying gods and goddesses. Their belief in these gruesome beings gave the Vikings courage in their bloody battles and raids. They believed that dying in battle would only help them go to a wonderful **afterlife**.

Thunderous Thor

Thor was the powerful god of thunder. The Vikings believed that a flash of lightning meant Thor had flung his hammer, which he used to overcome all evil and misbehaving giants!

Odin's ravens were also considered to be omens, or signs, of death.

One-Eyed Odin

Odin was the one-eyed god of thunder and lightning. Warriors who died in battle went to live with him. He carried a spear and rode an eight-legged horse. Odin had two ravens named Thought and Memory. These black birds flew around the world in the day and at night, and told Odin all they had seen.

Dark and Deadly!

Viking lives were full of danger so many Vikings wore lucky charms called amulets. The Vikings believed wearing an amulet in the shape of Thor's hammer would mean the god would protect them from evil.

Thor's hammer was a powerful amulet in Viking times.

Many Worlds

The Vikings believed that the world was made up of nine different realms, or worlds. Some of these worlds were ruled by terrifying gods, giants, dwarfs, and elves. These creatures controlled the worlds that they lived in.

Gods and Giants

Viking gods lived in a kingdom in the sky called Asgard. The Earth where humans lived was known as Midgard. Midgard was connected to Asgard by a rainbow bridge. Giants lived in an underworld and were the arch enemies of the gods.

The Vikings believed that during Ragnarök a giant wolf named Fenrir would kill the god Odin.

End of the World

The gods were there to fight the giants and other evil forces. The Vikings believed that the world would end with one dreadful, final battle between the gods and the giants known as Ragnarök. This struck fear into Viking hearts.

Dark and Deadly!

The Vikings believed that another of the nine worlds, Muspelheim, was a burning-hot place. It was home to terrible fire giants and fire demons and was filled with lava and flames. Vikings believed that the evil fire giant named Surt, who guarded the world of Muspelheim, would one day set fire to Asgard.

WHY DO YOU THINK THE VIKINGS BELIEVED THE WORLD WOULD END WITH ONE HUGE BATTLE?

This is an illustration of Muspelheim, where the Vikings believed fire demons and giants lived.

A Good Death

The Vikings believed that they would go to a great hall if they died well. The hall of the slain, or Valhalla, was where the bravest warriors went after they died. Valhalla was a great hall in Asgard, ruled over by the god Odin.

Fighting Fit in Heaven

Valhalla was a strange type of heaven! Vikings believed that during the day, dead warriors left Valhalla to fight viciously against each other. This was to keep them fighting fit and ready for the final battle between gods and giants.

Great female warriors known as Valkyries often feature in Viking stories. Valkyries were said to choose who would live or die in battles. They also decided what would happen to dead warriors.

Back to Life

After the fighting, the wounded warriors would be magically healed. Any warriors who had died in these scary battles would come to life again. Then they would return to Valhalla to spend the nights feasting and drinking.

Vikings believed a magical female goat named Heidrun sat on the roof of Valhalla, producing an alcoholic drink called mead, for the dead warriors to drink. Viking warriors drank mead from drinking horns, like this one.

Dark and Deadly!

Criminals who died faced a horrible afterlife. They went to a realm of darkness ruled over by the goddess Hel. There they were tormented by a bloodsucking dragon and a castle filled with poisonous serpents.

CHAPTER 6

LIFE AND DEATH

Death was just another part of life for the Vikings. They had little fear of it. That is probably because the Vikings faced death often. They experienced it on raids and in battles, and their large religious celebrations were often centered on death or **sacrifice**.

Happy Gods

The Vikings believed that it was important to keep their gods happy. To do this, they made regular sacrifices. The Vikings believed that in return for a sacrifice, the gods would make sure they got something they wanted, such as good weather or wealth.

Vikings often faced death, either in battle or from the hardship of life. Marking death was an important part of life for them.

Scary Sacrifices

A sacrifice usually took place during a feast or ceremony. Animals such as pigs and horses were often sacrificed. The meat was boiled in large cooking pits. Vikings believed blood from sacrifices had special powers, so they sprinkled it on statues of the gods and themselves. A feast and sacrifice could be dedicated to any of the gods. These festivals were sacred and important but also like parties.

Dark and Deadly!

Vikings greatly respected horses. They believed the animals could bring good luck, so horses were often sacrificed in a ceremony to ensure a good harvest or a successful raid. Vikings sacrificed horses to honor the gods, and then ate the horse meat at a feast.

Horses were important to the Vikings. They rode them into battle, and believed that they were strong and noble animals.

35

Super Sacrifices

For some Viking gods, an animal sacrifice was simply not good enough. Some gods demanded more. The Vikings believed that the god Odin would be satisfied only when humans were also put to death in his honor.

A Great Prize

Vikings believed a human life was the most valuable sacrifice that they could make to the gods. Some humans were sacrificed to the gods at religious festivals. These sacrifices took place in special buildings or outside in natural spaces that had been specially prepared for the ritual. At these ceremonies, prisoners of war were often sacrificed.

Slaves and prisoners of war had no control over what happened to them. They were often chosen as human sacrifices.

Dark and Deadly!

The Vikings performed a special ceremony at the temple at Uppsala, in Sweden, every nine years to keep the gods happy. It included the sacrifice of nine men in a holy **grove** nearby.

These Viking burial mounds are in Uppsala.

Different Deaths

The poor victims of sacrifices were killed in different ways. Some were strangled. Others were hit on the head or had their throat slit. Others were hanged from the trees—dead bodies have been found with the noose still around their necks.

Buried for Good

The afterlife was important to the Vikings. For that reason, Vikings were buried with all the belongings that their family would need in the afterlife. A warrior's most highly prized weapons were buried with him, and so were his unfortunate slaves. After a Viking was buried, piles of stone and soil were usually laid on top of the body.

Ships for the Rich

The wealthiest Vikings were buried in ships. Viking men had tools, clothing, weapons, and even money buried with them. Most Viking women spent their lives at home or on their farm, so they were buried with the things they would need in the afterlife. This included jewelry, bowls, knives, and cooking pots.

Masters and Slaves

Viking slaves were sometimes sacrificed when their masters died. They were often **beheaded** before being placed in the grave to be useful to their owner in the afterlife. A number of Viking warrior graves have been found to contain the remains of slaves.

Dark and Deadly!

The Oseberg is a Viking burial ship in which the bodies of two women were found. One was someone important, and the other woman was probably her slave.

Inside the Oseberg ship there were also the bones of 14 or 15 horses, a cat, birds, a bull, a cow, and four dogs.

THE VIKINGS BURIED SOME WOMEN WITH A LOT OF VALUABLE THINGS. WHAT DO YOU THINK THAT TELLS US ABOUT HOW THE VIKINGS VIEWED WOMEN?

Perhaps the woman buried in the Oseberg ship was a Viking leader.

Burning Brightly

A grave burial was not standard for all Vikings. Many were burned on a fire called a funeral pyre. The pyres could be very large, and flames from them could be seen far and wide. A vast amount of wood was used to ensure the blaze burned brightly.

Piled High

Most funeral pyres were on land. The body was dressed in fine clothes. Gifts and belongings were laid beside it on a pile of wooden logs, up to 65 feet (20 m) high. Animals, and sometimes people, were sacrificed and placed there, too. Then the fire was lit.

On to the Next Life

For the Vikings, boats were a symbol of safe passage into the afterlife. So sometimes, an important leader would be placed on his ship, which was then set alight. As it burned, it drifted out to sea as people watched on from the shore.

A Viking funeral ship must have been an amazing site for all who viewed it.

Dark and Deadly!

After a funeral pyre, people sifted through the ash and buried the remains of the body and the belongings, usually in an urn.

This is a Viking urn. Urns are containers that hold the ashes of people whose bodies have been cremated, or burned.

Nothing to Lose

Viking warriors risked their lives in battle without fear. That is because they believed their time of death was preordained, or already chosen. With nothing to lose, some Vikings became famous for the terror they wreaked when they were alive, and even more famous for their dramatic deaths!

A Great Viking

Ragnar Lodbrok was a legendary Viking raider. He led many of the brutal attacks on Paris and other parts of France and England. Lodbrok's nickname was Shaggy Breeches, because he wore trousers of animal fur. He is said to have been killed when an English king had him thrown into a pit of poisonous snakes.

Ragnar's success as a warrior made him a powerful lord among the Vikings.

Legendary Lagertha

Lagertha was a shieldmaiden. This was a female Viking warrior. Lagertha was one of the most famous shieldmaidens. She dressed in men's clothing to fight fearlessly against Lodbrok's enemies. Lagertha was said to have had the courage of a man and fought among the bravest.

Rune stones were erected to remember and celebrate the most infamous Viking warriors, such as Ragnar Lodbrok.

Dark and Deadly!

History's most horrible Vikings had nicknames that were as bloodcurdling as the men themselves, such as Eric Bloodaxe, Sigurd Snake-in-the-Eye, and Ivar the Boneless.

END OF THE VIKINGS

The Vikings were vicious raiders and brutal warriors. They were an incredible fighting force, and feared by all who encountered them. But their reign of terror could not go on forever.

Tired of Terror

Over time, people had grown tired of the Vikings' power. They began to fight back, and grouped together to defend themselves against Viking attacks. Vikings lost savage fights for control in many countries. The last Viking king of York, Eric Bloodaxe, was expelled from Northumbria in 954 CE.

Dark and Deadly!

The Vikings are famous for being bloodthirsty killers, but there is proof that by the end of the Viking age, many had left behind their murderous ways. Viking rune stones called the Jelling stones have a figure of Jesus Christ on the cross on them—a sign that the Vikings had become Christians and were no longer seafaring warriors.

No More Fight

By the twelfth century, most Vikings had settled down. Many became Christians and forgot their old Viking gods. The age of the mighty and murderous Vikings was over.

Eventually, many Vikings gave up their weapons and settled in places where growing crops and raising livestock was easier.

The Jelling stones were erected in memory of a king's parents. Rune stones like this were erected near roads or bridges, so that many Vikings could see them.

GLOSSARY

afterlife life after death. Some people believe that after we die we go to live in another world

Anglo-Saxon describes English history from the fifth century CE to the Norman Conquest in 1066

antler a deer horn

bacteria tiny living things that can help waste decay, or rot

beheaded killed by cutting off the person's head

chain mail armor made of small metal rings linked together

conquer to use force to take over a city or country

fermented food that contains beneficial bacteria

figureheads wooden carvings at the front of ships

friction the force that makes it difficult for things to move freely when they are touching each other

grove a group of trees that are close together

inherit to receive something from someone who has died

invaders people, armies, or countries that use force to enter and take control of another country

lethal deadly

manuscripts handwritten documents

mass grave a grave in which many bodies are buried together

menacing describes something that causes harm or danger

monastery a building or group of buildings where monks live

monks holy men who devote their life to their Christian religion and live with other monks in a monastery

Norse the language of ancient Norway, Sweden, and Denmark

opponents people fighting against another army or group

plunder to steal from a place

rune stones stones with runes, letters from the Viking alphabet, carved into them

sacrifice killed to honor a god or gods

Scandinavia the group of countries that includes Denmark, Norway, and Sweden

settlements places where people have built homes

slaves people who are owned by other people and have to obey them

FIND OUT MORE

Books

Alexander, Heather and Meredith Hamilton. *A Child's Introduction to Norse Mythology: Odin, Thor, Loki, and Other Viking Gods, Goddesses, Giants, and Monsters.* Black Dog & Leventhal, 2018.

Bailey, Linda. *Stowing Away with the Vikings* (Time Travel Guides). Kids Can Press, 2018.

Yomtove, Nel. V*ikings: Scandinavia's Ferocious Sea Raiders.* Capstone Publishing Company, 2019.

Websites

Discover more about the Vikings at:
www.ducksters.com/history/middle_ages_vikings.php

Find out about Viking children at:
**https://en.natmus.dk/historical-knowledge/denmark/prehistoric-
period-until-1050-ad/the-viking-age/thepeople/children**

Learn more Viking facts at:
**www.natgeokids.com/uk/discover/history/generalhistory/
10-facts-about-the-vikings**

Publisher's note to educators and parents:
All the websites featured above have been carefully reviewed to ensure that they are suitable for students. However, many websites change often, and we cannot guarantee that a site's future contents will continue to meet our high standards of educational value. Please be advised that students should be closely monitored whenever they access the Internet

INDEX

About the Authors
Sarah Eason and Louise Spilsbury
have written many history books
for children. Both love finding out
about past people, and through
writing this book have learned
how deadly daily life really was
for people who lived during the
age of the violent Vikings.